EMMANUEL JOSEPH

Nurturing Young Innovators, Cultivating Morality and Faith in Future Entrepreneurs

Copyright © 2025 by Emmanuel Joseph

All rights reserved. No part of this publication may be reproduced, stored or transmitted in any form or by any means, electronic, mechanical, photocopying, recording, scanning, or otherwise without written permission from the publisher. It is illegal to copy this book, post it to a website, or distribute it by any other means without permission.

First edition

This book was professionally typeset on Reedsy. Find out more at reedsy.com

Contents

1	Chapter 1	1
2	Chapter 1: The Seed of Innovation	4
3	Chapter 2: The Spark of Curiosity	6
4	Chapter 3: The Spirit of Collaboration	8
5	Chapter 4: The Role of Mentorship	10
6	Chapter 5: Bridging Tradition and Innovation	12
7	Chapter 6: Embracing Challenges	14
8	Chapter 7: The Balance of Morality	16
9	Chapter 8: The Importance of Faith	17
10	Chapter 9: The Power of Community	18
11	Chapter 10: Overcoming Adversity	19
12	Chapter 11: Embracing Diversity	20
13	Chapter 12: The Pursuit of Sustainability	21
14	Chapter 13: The Role of Education	22
15	Chapter 14: Building a Legacy	23
16	Chapter 15: The Future of Innovation	24

1

Chapter 1

Introduction

Innovation is the lifeblood of progress, driving society forward and transforming the way we live, work, and interact. In a rapidly changing world, fostering a spirit of innovation among the younger generation is more crucial than ever. However, true innovation goes beyond mere technological advancements; it encompasses the cultivation of morality and faith, guiding young minds to create solutions that are not only ingenious but also ethically sound and socially responsible. This book, "Nurturing Young Innovators: Cultivating Morality and Faith in Future Entrepreneurs," delves into the journey of fostering innovation with a strong moral compass.

The story of Olu, a young innovator from Lagos, Nigeria, serves as a compelling narrative that illustrates the multifaceted nature of innovation. Olu's journey is a testament to the power of curiosity, resilience, and collaboration. From his humble beginnings, tinkering with discarded materials, to developing groundbreaking solutions that benefit his community, Olu's experiences highlight the importance of nurturing young talent and providing the right environment for innovation to flourish.

Central to Olu's journey is the role of mentorship and community support. The guidance and encouragement he receives from mentors, parents, and peers play a pivotal role in shaping his path. This book underscores the significance of creating supportive ecosystems where young innovators can thrive. It emphasizes the need for collaboration, diverse perspectives, and the collective wisdom that emerges when individuals come together with a shared vision. Olu's story demonstrates that innovation is not a solitary endeavor but a communal effort that requires trust, respect, and mutual support.

The book also explores the intersection of tradition and innovation, illustrating how cultural heritage can inspire and enrich modern solutions. Olu's ability to integrate traditional practices with contemporary technology showcases the potential for innovation to honor and preserve cultural identity. This harmonious blend of the past and the future serves as a reminder that innovation need not come at the expense of tradition. Instead, it can draw strength and inspiration from it, creating solutions that are both innovative and culturally relevant.

Another key theme is the importance of faith and morality in the innovation process. Olu's journey is guided by a strong sense of purpose and ethical considerations. He learns to navigate the complexities of innovation with integrity, understanding that his work should benefit society and uphold the values he holds dear. This book highlights the need for young innovators to cultivate a moral compass that guides their actions and decisions. It emphasizes that true innovation is not just about creating new products but about making a positive impact on the world.

Throughout the book, readers will find practical insights and lessons that can be applied to their own journeys of innovation. The stories and experiences shared serve as a source of inspiration and guidance for aspiring entrepreneurs. Whether it's overcoming challenges, embracing diversity, or balancing tradition with modernity, Olu's journey offers valuable lessons that can help young innovators navigate their own paths. This book aims to equip readers with the tools and mindset needed to pursue innovation with confidence and purpose.

In essence, "Nurturing Young Innovators: Cultivating Morality and Faith in Future Entrepreneurs" is a celebration of the potential within each young mind. It is a call to action for educators, parents, mentors, and communities to invest in the future by nurturing the innovators of tomorrow. Through the

CHAPTER 1

lens of Olu's journey, this book provides a roadmap for fostering innovation that is rooted in morality, guided by faith, and driven by a commitment to making the world a better place. It is an invitation to embark on a journey of discovery, creativity, and impact, shaping a brighter future for all.

2

Chapter 1: The Seed of Innovation

The bustling streets of Lagos were teeming with life as Olu ventured out for his daily walk. He was a young boy with a mind that never stopped whirring—always curious, always questioning. His love for tinkering with gadgets often landed him in trouble, but it also sparked a fire within him. It was on one of these walks that he stumbled upon an old, abandoned workshop. The dilapidated building, once a thriving hub of creativity, now stood as a relic of past innovation. As Olu explored the dusty remnants of forgotten projects, he felt a spark of inspiration. He realized that innovation was not just about creating new gadgets but also about breathing new life into old ideas.

Olu's journey of innovation began with a simple question: "What if?" What if he could transform discarded materials into something useful? What if he could solve everyday problems with ingenious solutions? As he rummaged through the piles of scrap, he found an old bicycle frame, a broken radio, and a collection of rusty gears. With a determined glint in his eye, he decided to rebuild the bicycle using the discarded parts. It was a challenging task, but Olu's determination and resourcefulness saw him through. As he pedaled his newly rebuilt bicycle through the streets, he felt a sense of accomplishment and pride. His journey had just begun.

The seed of innovation had been planted, but it needed nurturing. Olu's parents, recognizing his potential, encouraged him to pursue his passion.

CHAPTER 1: THE SEED OF INNOVATION

They enrolled him in a local makerspace, where he met like-minded individuals and mentors who shared his enthusiasm. The makerspace became a haven for Olu, a place where he could experiment, learn, and grow. It was here that he realized the importance of collaboration and community in the process of innovation. Surrounded by a supportive network, Olu's ideas flourished, and he began to see the world through a lens of possibility.

Innovation, however, is not just about creating new things; it is also about cultivating a sense of morality and faith. Olu's parents instilled in him the values of honesty, integrity, and empathy. They taught him that true innovation should aim to make the world a better place. As Olu's projects grew in complexity, he faced ethical dilemmas and challenges. He learned that innovation without a moral compass could lead to unintended consequences. Through introspection and guidance from his mentors, Olu developed a strong sense of responsibility. He understood that his inventions should benefit society and uphold the values he held dear.

3

Chapter 2: The Spark of Curiosity

One afternoon, while exploring the markets of Lagos, Olu came across a peculiar stall that sold odd trinkets and mysterious gadgets. His eyes were immediately drawn to an ancient-looking compass that seemed to have a life of its own. The stall owner, an elderly man with a long, white beard, noticed Olu's fascination and decided to share the story behind the compass. He explained that the compass had once belonged to a great explorer who had discovered many hidden treasures. Intrigued by the tale, Olu purchased the compass, believing it to be more than just an old relic. This curiosity marked the beginning of his quest for knowledge and discovery.

With the compass in hand, Olu began to explore new ideas and concepts. He found himself drawn to the mysteries of science, technology, and the natural world. He spent countless hours reading books, watching documentaries, and experimenting with different materials. Each new discovery fueled his passion and opened up new avenues for exploration. His inquisitive nature led him to question the world around him, always seeking to understand the "why" and "how" of things. This insatiable curiosity became the driving force behind his innovative spirit.

Olu's journey of discovery was not without its challenges. He often faced skepticism and doubt from those who did not share his vision. However, he remained undeterred, driven by an inner conviction that his ideas had the power to change the world. One day, while experimenting with solar panels, Olu stumbled upon a breakthrough. He discovered a way to make the panels more efficient, harnessing the power of the sun to generate electricity for his community. This achievement not only validated his efforts but also earned him recognition and support from his peers and mentors.

As Olu's reputation as a young innovator grew, he began to attract the attention of local entrepreneurs and investors. They saw in him a promising talent with the potential to bring about meaningful change. One such entrepreneur, a successful businesswoman named Aisha, took Olu under her wing. She introduced him to the world of business and entrepreneurship, teaching him valuable lessons about leadership, management, and perseverance. With her guidance, Olu learned to navigate the complexities of the business world while staying true to his values and vision.

Olu's journey was not just about personal success; it was about making a difference in the lives of others. He began to see innovation as a means to address the pressing challenges faced by his community. He understood that true innovation was not just about creating new products but also about finding sustainable solutions to real-world problems. With this newfound perspective, Olu dedicated himself to projects that would improve the quality of life for those around him. His work became a testament to the power of curiosity, determination, and the unwavering belief in a better future.

4

Chapter 3: The Spirit of Collaboration

At the heart of Olu's journey was the realization that innovation did not happen in isolation. It was within the lively walls of the makerspace that he truly experienced the power of collaboration. Here, individuals from different backgrounds and areas of expertise came together to share ideas and work on projects. Olu quickly learned that innovation thrived in an environment where diverse perspectives were valued and collective wisdom was harnessed. His project on sustainable energy solutions attracted attention and soon, he was working with a team of engineers, scientists, and fellow tinkerers, each bringing their unique skills to the table.

The team's first major project was to design and build solar-powered streetlights for their community. It was an ambitious endeavor that required meticulous planning, creativity, and perseverance. There were moments of frustration and setbacks, but through it all, Olu and his team remained united by a shared vision. They held regular brainstorming sessions, where no idea was too wild or impractical. Through open dialogue and constructive feedback, they refined their designs and overcame technical challenges. The project was a testament to the power of collaboration, proving that together, they could achieve far more than any one individual could alone.

As the solar-powered streetlights began to illuminate the streets of Lagos, the impact of the project was palpable. The community, once plagued by

CHAPTER 3: THE SPIRIT OF COLLABORATION

frequent power outages, now had a reliable source of light that enhanced safety and security. Olu's team was celebrated as local heroes, and their success inspired others to dream big and work together towards a common goal. The project also highlighted the importance of community engagement. Olu and his team regularly sought input from residents, ensuring that the solutions they developed were tailored to the community's needs and preferences.

Olu's experience with collaborative innovation taught him valuable lessons about leadership and teamwork. He realized that effective leaders were those who could inspire and empower others, rather than dictate and control. Olu adopted a servant-leadership approach, always listening to his team members and valuing their contributions. He fostered a culture of trust and mutual respect, where everyone's voice was heard. This inclusive environment not only boosted team morale but also led to more creative and effective solutions. Through collaboration, Olu discovered that innovation was not just about individual brilliance but about harnessing the collective genius of a diverse group.

5

Chapter 4: The Role of Mentorship

In Olu's journey, mentors played a crucial role in shaping his growth and development as an innovator. From his parents, who nurtured his early curiosity, to the mentors he met at the makerspace, each one left an indelible mark on his path. A key mentor was Dr. Ifeanyi, a renowned engineer and entrepreneur who had dedicated his life to fostering young talent. Dr. Ifeanyi saw great potential in Olu and took him under his wing. He provided guidance, shared his wealth of knowledge, and challenged Olu to think critically and push the boundaries of what was possible.

Under Dr. Ifeanyi's mentorship, Olu was introduced to the principles of design thinking and human-centered design. He learned to approach problems from the perspective of the end-user, always considering their needs, challenges, and aspirations. This shift in mindset transformed the way Olu approached innovation. He began to see technology not just as a tool but as a means to improve people's lives. Dr. Ifeanyi also encouraged Olu to embrace failure as a learning opportunity. He taught him that setbacks were an inevitable part of the innovation process and that resilience and perseverance were key to success.

One of the most memorable lessons Olu learned from Dr. Ifeanyi was the importance of giving back. Dr. Ifeanyi often spoke about the concept of "paying it forward" and the responsibility of successful innovators to mentor and support the next generation. Inspired by this ethos, Olu started a mentorship program at the makerspace, where he worked with younger students who shared his passion for innovation. He found great fulfillment in helping others unlock their potential and realize their dreams. Through mentorship, Olu discovered the true impact of his work extended beyond his individual achievements—it was about creating a legacy of innovation and empowerment.

The mentorship program grew, attracting students from all over Lagos who were eager to learn and innovate. Olu's journey had come full circle. He was now a mentor, guiding and inspiring the next generation of young innovators. The program fostered a supportive community where knowledge and experiences were shared freely. Olu's mentees not only gained technical skills but also developed a strong sense of purpose and responsibility. They understood that innovation was not just about personal success but about making a positive impact on society. Through mentorship, Olu was able to pass on the values and lessons he had learned, ensuring that the spirit of innovation continued to thrive.

6

Chapter 5: Bridging Tradition and Innovation

One of the unique aspects of Olu's journey was his ability to bridge the gap between tradition and innovation. Growing up in Nigeria, he was deeply rooted in his cultural heritage, which shaped his values and worldview. He realized that while innovation often involved new technologies and ideas, it could also draw inspiration from traditional practices and wisdom. This realization led him to explore how modern innovation could be harmonized with cultural traditions to create solutions that were both innovative and respectful of heritage.

One of Olu's projects involved working with local artisans to integrate traditional craftsmanship with modern technology. He collaborated with skilled weavers and potters, learning about their techniques and the cultural significance behind their crafts. Together, they developed a line of products that combined traditional aesthetics with contemporary functionality. For example, they created solar-powered lanterns that were adorned with intricate patterns inspired by traditional Nigerian art. These products not only showcased the beauty of Nigerian culture but also provided practical solutions for everyday use.

Olu's work in bridging tradition and innovation extended to agriculture as well. He saw the potential to enhance traditional farming practices with

CHAPTER 5: BRIDGING TRADITION AND INNOVATION

modern technology to improve efficiency and sustainability. He introduced smart irrigation systems and solar-powered equipment to local farmers, helping them increase their yield and reduce their reliance on manual labor. By respecting and building upon traditional knowledge, Olu was able to create solutions that were both effective and culturally relevant. His projects demonstrated that innovation did not have to come at the expense of tradition; rather, the two could coexist and enrich each other.

Olu's ability to bridge tradition and innovation earned him admiration and respect from both the older and younger generations. He became a symbol of how progress could be achieved without losing one's cultural identity. His projects inspired a sense of pride and ownership within the community, showing that innovation could be a means to preserve and celebrate cultural heritage. Through his work, Olu demonstrated that the past and the future were not mutually exclusive; instead, they could be woven together to create a richer, more vibrant tapestry of innovation.

7

Chapter 6: Embracing Challenges

Olu's journey was marked by numerous challenges and obstacles that tested his resilience and determination. Each challenge he faced was a learning opportunity that helped him grow as an innovator and as a person. One of the most significant challenges came in the form of a major project that involved developing a low-cost water purification system for rural communities. The project was ambitious and required extensive research, testing, and collaboration with experts in various fields.

The initial stages of the project were fraught with difficulties. The team encountered technical issues, funding constraints, and logistical hurdles. There were moments of doubt and frustration, but Olu remained steadfast in his commitment to the project. He rallied his team, encouraging them to stay focused on their goal and to view challenges as opportunities for growth. Through perseverance and creative problem-solving, the team overcame each obstacle, gradually making progress.

One of the key breakthroughs came when Olu and his team discovered a cost-effective method of using locally sourced materials for the purification system. This innovation not only reduced the overall cost but also made the system more accessible and sustainable for rural communities. The team's dedication and hard work paid off when they successfully implemented the water purification system in several villages, providing clean and safe drinking water to thousands of people. The project was a testament to the power of

CHAPTER 6: EMBRACING CHALLENGES

resilience and the belief that even the most daunting challenges could be overcome with determination and creativity.

Olu's experience with the water purification project reinforced his belief that challenges were an integral part of the innovation process. He learned that setbacks and failures were not indicators of defeat but rather stepping stones to success. Each challenge he faced helped him develop new skills, gain valuable insights, and build a stronger character. Olu's journey was a reminder that true innovation required the courage to embrace challenges and the resilience to keep moving forward, no matter how difficult the path might be.

8

Chapter 7: The Balance of Morality

As Olu's projects gained momentum, he was faced with ethical dilemmas that tested his moral compass. One such dilemma arose when a multinational corporation expressed interest in his solar-powered streetlight technology. While the partnership promised significant financial rewards and global recognition, it also meant relinquishing control over his invention. Olu wrestled with the decision, weighing the potential benefits against the risk of his technology being used in ways that could harm communities or exploit resources.

After much contemplation and seeking advice from his mentors, Olu decided to turn down the offer. He realized that maintaining his integrity and staying true to his values were more important than financial gain. This decision reinforced his belief that innovation should be guided by a strong moral foundation. Olu continued to develop his projects with a focus on ethical considerations, ensuring that his work contributed positively to society. His commitment to morality earned him respect and admiration, setting an example for other young innovators to follow.

Chapter 8: The Importance of Faith

Faith played a significant role in Olu's journey, providing him with strength and guidance during challenging times. Raised in a family that valued spirituality, Olu learned to draw on his faith for inspiration and resilience. His belief in a higher purpose gave him the courage to pursue his dreams and the conviction that his work had a greater meaning. Olu's faith also shaped his interactions with others, fostering a sense of compassion, empathy, and humility.

One particular instance where faith guided Olu was during a critical point in his water purification project. Faced with technical setbacks and dwindling resources, Olu felt overwhelmed and uncertain about the future of the project. In a moment of introspection, he turned to his faith for solace and clarity. Through prayer and meditation, he found renewed strength and a sense of calm. This spiritual grounding allowed him to approach the challenges with a clear mind and an unwavering resolve. The project eventually succeeded, and Olu credited his faith for helping him navigate the difficult times.

10

Chapter 9: The Power of Community

Throughout his journey, Olu recognized the profound impact of community support. The makerspace, local entrepreneurs, and mentors all played crucial roles in his development. Olu understood that innovation was not just about individual brilliance but about creating a supportive ecosystem where ideas could flourish. He actively engaged with his community, sharing his knowledge and experiences while also learning from others.

One of Olu's most rewarding experiences was organizing community workshops where he taught young students about innovation and entrepreneurship. These workshops became a platform for aspiring innovators to explore their potential and gain practical skills. The sense of camaraderie and shared purpose fueled Olu's passion for giving back. He witnessed firsthand how a strong community could empower individuals and drive collective progress. The workshops also fostered a culture of collaboration and mutual support, creating a network of innovators who were committed to making a positive impact.

11

Chapter 10: Overcoming Adversity

Olu's journey was not without its share of adversity. He faced numerous setbacks, from technical failures to funding challenges. However, each obstacle he encountered strengthened his resolve and resilience. One significant adversity arose when a key investor withdrew support for one of his projects, leaving Olu and his team scrambling for resources.

Instead of giving up, Olu rallied his team and explored alternative funding sources. They organized crowdfunding campaigns, reached out to local businesses, and sought grants from non-profit organizations. Through their collective efforts, they managed to secure the necessary funds to continue the project. This experience taught Olu the importance of adaptability and resourcefulness. It also reinforced his belief that true innovation required the ability to persevere through adversity and remain committed to one's vision.

12

Chapter 11: Embracing Diversity

Olu learned early on that diversity was a strength, not a hindrance. His experiences at the makerspace exposed him to individuals from different cultural, educational, and professional backgrounds. This diversity enriched his perspective and sparked new ideas. Olu realized that innovative solutions often emerged from the intersection of diverse viewpoints. He actively sought out collaboration with people who brought different skills, experiences, and perspectives to the table.

One project that exemplified the power of diversity was the development of an affordable healthcare device. Olu and his team worked with healthcare professionals, engineers, designers, and patients to create a solution that was both effective and user-friendly. The diverse inputs ensured that the device addressed a wide range of needs and considerations. The project highlighted the value of inclusivity and the importance of creating an environment where everyone's voice was heard. Olu's commitment to diversity became a cornerstone of his approach to innovation.

13

Chapter 12: The Pursuit of Sustainability

Sustainability became a central theme in Olu's work as he recognized the pressing need to address environmental challenges. He believed that innovation should not come at the expense of the planet's health. This conviction led him to explore sustainable practices and develop eco-friendly solutions. One notable project involved creating biodegradable packaging materials using local agricultural waste.

The project was a collaborative effort with local farmers, scientists, and entrepreneurs. Together, they developed a process to convert waste materials into durable and environmentally friendly packaging. The initiative not only reduced waste but also provided additional income for farmers. Olu's work in sustainability earned him recognition and awards, but more importantly, it demonstrated that innovation could be both economically viable and environmentally responsible.

14

Chapter 13: The Role of Education

Education was a driving force in Olu's journey. His thirst for knowledge and his desire to learn fueled his passion for innovation. Olu recognized that education was the key to unlocking potential and empowering individuals. He actively sought opportunities to further his education, attending workshops, seminars, and online courses. Olu also believed in the power of experiential learning, gaining hands-on experience through his projects and collaborations.

One of Olu's initiatives was to improve access to quality education in underserved communities. He worked with local schools to develop science and technology programs that engaged students and sparked their interest in innovation. The programs included hands-on activities, guest lectures from industry professionals, and field trips to tech companies. Olu's efforts created a ripple effect, inspiring a new generation of young innovators who were eager to explore and create. His work highlighted the transformative power of education and the importance of providing opportunities for all.

15

Chapter 14: Building a Legacy

As Olu's reputation as an innovator grew, he began to think about his legacy. He wanted his work to have a lasting impact and to inspire future generations. Olu's mentorship program, community workshops, and educational initiatives were all part of his efforts to build a legacy of innovation and empowerment. He understood that his greatest contribution was not just his inventions but the values and principles he instilled in others.

Olu's journey came full circle when he was invited to speak at a global innovation summit. He shared his story, emphasizing the importance of morality, faith, and community in the innovation process. Olu's message resonated with the audience, inspiring many to pursue their own paths of innovation with integrity and purpose. His legacy was not just about the technological solutions he created but about the spirit of innovation and the positive change he championed.

16

Chapter 15: The Future of Innovation

Olu's journey was just the beginning. As he looked to the future, he saw endless possibilities for innovation and progress. He envisioned a world where young innovators, guided by strong values and a sense of purpose, would tackle the challenges of tomorrow. Olu continued to mentor and support aspiring innovators, sharing his knowledge and experiences. He remained committed to his vision of creating a better world through innovation, driven by morality, faith, and community.

Olu's story was a testament to the power of perseverance, curiosity, and collaboration. It demonstrated that innovation was not just about creating new technologies but about making a positive impact on society. As he stood at the threshold of the future, Olu was filled with hope and excitement. He knew that the journey of innovation was never-ending and that each step forward was a step towards a brighter, more sustainable, and more inclusive world.

Book Description:

In a world driven by rapid technological advancements and ever-evolving challenges, the need to nurture young innovators has never been more crucial. "Nurturing Young Innovators: Cultivating Morality and Faith in Future Entrepreneurs" delves into the essence of fostering innovation that is rooted in strong ethical values and guided by a sense of purpose. Through the captivating story of Olu, a young and ambitious innovator from Lagos,

CHAPTER 15: THE FUTURE OF INNOVATION

Nigeria, this book explores the multifaceted journey of creativity, resilience, and social responsibility.

Olu's tale is one of discovery, determination, and transformation. From his early days of tinkering with discarded gadgets to developing groundbreaking solutions for his community, Olu's experiences serve as a beacon of inspiration for aspiring entrepreneurs. His journey is enriched by the guidance of mentors, the support of his community, and the wisdom drawn from his cultural heritage. Through collaborative projects, ethical decision-making, and embracing challenges, Olu learns that true innovation goes beyond technological prowess—it is about making a positive impact on society.

This book weaves together engaging stories and practical insights that highlight the importance of morality and faith in the innovation process. It underscores the significance of mentorship, community support, and the harmonious blend of tradition and modernity. Readers will be inspired by Olu's ability to navigate ethical dilemmas, his unwavering commitment to sustainability, and his efforts to create solutions that are both innovative and culturally relevant.

"Nurturing Young Innovators" is a call to action for educators, parents, mentors, and communities to invest in the future by cultivating the next generation of innovators. It provides a roadmap for fostering creativity, ethical leadership, and a sense of purpose in young minds. Through Olu's journey, readers will discover the power of curiosity, collaboration, and perseverance in shaping a brighter and more inclusive future. This book is a testament to the potential within each young individual and the transformative impact they can have on the world when guided by strong moral values and faith.

www.ingramcontent.com/pod-product-compliance
Lightning Source LLC
LaVergne TN
LVHW020743090526
838202LV00057BA/6213